Penguin Coloring Book for Kids

Cute and Easy Colouring Book for Toddler and Kids

by Nick Marshall

Copyright © 2020 by Nick Marshall All rights reserved.
No part of this book may be reproduced in any form or by any electronic or mechanical means, including information storage and retrieval systems, without written permission from the author, except for the use of brief quotations in a book review.

This Coloring Book Belongs to

_____

Made in the USA
Columbia, SC
29 November 2023